An Inch or So of Garden
. *Poems 1968-1972*
Homecomings: Narrative Poems
Divinations and Shorter Poems, 1973-1978
Walking Under the Nebulae
Reckonings: Poems 1979-1985
Solid Things

Temporary Shelter

Poems 1986-1990

M. Travis Lane

GOOSE LANE

Published by Goose Lane Editions with the assistance of the Canada Council and the New Brunswick Department of Municipalities, Culture and Housing, 1993.

Publications in which these poems have appeared: *The Antigonish Review, Arc, The Canadian Forum, Canadian Literature, Cormorant, Event, Exile, Fiddlehead, The New Quarterly, Northward Journal, Other Voices, The Pottersfield Portfolio, Quarry, Room of One's Own, Scrivener, Tidepool.*

Cover photograph "Red Fox in a Cemetery" © Wendy Shattil/ Bob Rozinski, 1988.
Book design by Brenda Steeves.
Printed and bound in Canada by The Tribune Press.

Canadian Cataloguing in Publication Data

Lane, M. Travis (Millicent Travis), 1934-
    Temporary shelter
    Poems.
    ISBN 0-86492-148-9

I. Title.

PS8573.A55T56 1993   C811'.54   C93-098516-8
PR9199.3.L3T56 1993

Goose Lane Editions
469 King Street
Fredericton, New Brunswick
Canada E3B 1E5

To friends and family

Contents

Structuring Miscellany

The order of the separate poems in a poet's collection may be meaningful. A book may be composed of one or more sets of variations upon themes, or as a chronologically paced diary, or as a narrative or argumentative sequence. This collection, *Temporary Shelter*, has no such order.

I am not ordering these poems by theme because I do not write poems about themes. I am not ordering these poems by imagery because I write with, not about, imagery. One image may differently serve several different ideas. Grouping poems with similar imagery may cause the reader to mistake image for subject. "You'll just keep on painting that haystack until you get it right, eh, Monet?" My subject is always the emotional experience of thought, but not, however, always the same thought.

And this book is no diary. I am under revision but have not grown wiser. And my poems do not build upon each other like coral polyps in a reef. Each of these poems is a separate experience. To force progressive or developmental structure on a miscellany of discrete amusements is to forsake the fact of poetry for the wish of theory. Where poems are not linked, they must be read as separate.

The three long poems of this collection, "Local Suite," "Dear Tiger," and "Hills," have in common with each other only what they have in common with most Western poetry: their origin in solitude, their impetus in meditation upon the inescapable issues of human existence, and whatever the reader provides.

What one reader sees as Jungian archetype another sees as reference to the insecurities of extratextual reality. One image can be both. And the poems share my own skepticism toward some conventional values. "Local Suite" might be read as questioning our tendency to suppose smallness less serious than largeness. "Dear Tiger" asks if names forgotten are less important than names remembered. "Hills" disvalues the adventure of inscribing self upon or against nature.

But "Local Suite" has no feminism, wilderness, philosophy, or characterization. The sequence was an experiment, to see how minimally I could write and still please myself. The poem refuses to work out its metaphors, poses no ideas, develops no narrative, and avoids the personal. Constructed like programme music, representing a sequence of moods conventionally related to time of day and season, it relies on the subtleties of minor emotions.

"Dear Tiger," on the other hand, in which the landscape of place and season figures less, is a set of three female voices that make three feminist points: that Woman is defined as image, as that which is looked at; that Woman has defined herself primarily in terms of the male figures of her experience; and that Woman has no story. She is nameless, unheard, forgotten, unread.

"Hills" is also feminist, but its heroine, though unvoiced in the poem, has great vitality. She is dead but lives still. "Hills" thinks about our relation to nature and wilderness and about the ways in which we recall, misrecall, and invent our realities. The desire to order our apprehensions of nature is identified in the poem with the masculine and opposed to the approach, seen in the poem as feminine, of simply living in flux, immersed, accepting, unstructuring. The poem celebrates the open against the enclosed, the wilderness against the city, the imagination against tidily nailing things down. Yet it is wrong to insist that the imposition of order upon nature is masculine. Housewife Eve also named animals.

When Adrienne Rich writes of meaning searching for its word like a hermit crab its shell, she makes more poignant Robert Frost's image of metaphor as a temporary and imprecisely fitting shelter against the confusion of experience. Both poets remind us that the word is not the meaning nor is the word created by the meaning. The shell may be discarded. But a shell, a word, is needed. Unhoused, the nude crab perishes.

The illuminations of philosophy are not math but poetry, neither precise nor irrefutable. Theory is only narrative, myth, extended metaphor. An image is no equation. At present, resistance like mine to theory is often characterized as either Anglo-Saxon or as feminine. In me it is largely Emersonian, pragmatic, transcendentalist, a function of reason.

I have arranged the poems in this book as I might flowers in a vase, not in an order, but with an eye to balance, grace and variation. Read them in what order you like. They are not nailed down.

You Want Your Truths Told of You

You want your truths told of you —
    those wavery lines!
        Each pencil mark's a fiddlehead
            unfolding to an island of wild fern,
of alders, grass, of willow trees,
    of sharp clams in the silty sand
        where a barefoot girl
            stands to watch a cattle barge
rock, like a cradle in the wind.

She can not tell them where she stands,
    her nude toes turning blue as clams
        in the murky water where it chafes
            the green facts into islands —
shoals, reefs, whirlpools, naked trees
    scoured by the ice.
        Her plain nouns bell their inner folds
          like a coiled spring uncoiling
          or like eggs

that tremble in her hand and beat
    their shells with razor bills and spread
        out wings.
Their shadows cast on the millstream float
    on spinning water for all time,
        never entirely truthful.

Ave Maters

May the gentle, unrecorded saints
in their unmapped progressions make
a dial around the minutes of my hand
and help me write.
                    Black stars,
they draw me through their sieves,
through their forgotten histories,
seeing the world from inside out:
        mum matter, anti-matter moms —
            the flipside of
                        OM   OM

Windfall

The sudden drop of the peak wind:
    stone into valley —

a silence rebounds
     from the rock-slides rounding
       the hollow
          fall.

Echo of
      breathing —

            the trees below

sharp

   the glaciers
        humming
   the rocks
       steaming —

Hills

1.

My grandfather pencilled a skyline map:
from Pike's to Long's, each mountain's name.
We told them like a rosary.
Childhood, which seems to us so clear,
made as it is of stories, is a myth.
We map the past with images.
The lines grow simpler as we age.

One after one my mountains have gone west,
have faded into the evenings, all
those mountain women, those white heads.

And you, who first meant "mountain" to my life,
come to me now, as a sequential image —
not real (the real belongs to God) —
but her I have forgotten and resaid.

Cast to the rise. If I
tickle the surface of this lake
will a ghost leap, silver?
From the moon-tipped crescent of a peak
can I invoke one shadow?
                    When I stand
a candle in a dark room, in that flame
a spirit circles like a moth
caught in a single image: she
who cooked by candle all winter long
in the mountain's light.

2.
At first she was only a mountain place,
her dipper a kindergarten grail,
but stories cast around her a dark lure:
disease, divorce, a brother's death. I gnawed
these fragments into legend, a doubledness
divided, healed, a mind
that shed belief, hope, human ties,
set out toward mountain solitudes
as if the shining of one star, one solitary candle,
were enough.

The great brass bed
heaped with its chilly comforters
has filled with dust. The moon,
seeping between the plastered logs,
has touched the sepia photograph
of the twins in their white, old-fashioned clothes.
    Younger than me. The boy is dead.
    The other is her. She had polio.

When did I first imagine it:
her brother built the cabin, he, twin,
double, dead — and that
beyond the snow-enkindled lake
(small as a puddle, in memory
a sea, with Sawtooth upside down
suspended in its milky way) —
over the ridge with its bear-clawed spruce
was the lover, the hater, the separate man
once double and twin as husband and now dead

in having no more story — there
was his secret pasture, his iron gate,
barbed wire, a cattle grate, and locked
barns empty of living things. No lights,
no voices, "No Trespassing."

Her cabin was never locked. The key
hung by the door like a blessing, and the room
her brother started for himself
lay incomplete beyond her hearth, unroofed
and open to the sky . . .

3.
Maps, trails, houses, poetry —
he wrote his name on every log.
For her the trees were word enough, the open poem,
the wilderness. His choice, not hers, the tighter knot,
the involuted masterpiece worked back
into the crevices, rose gulch, the scent of raspberries,
lode, vein, and darkened cave.

She followed the outcrops of the rock, the paths
deer make to their lookouts —
always the high places, the wide air.
We choose the allegories of our selves,
his niche, his distillations — she
refused a year spent flat in bed
and the corset back.

                                    As a beast will gnaw
a trapped paw free,
she chose immediate freedom, lame.

He was not best man at her wedding, shade
by then. Without his maps and structures was she lost?
How had she mistaken this mind for his?
This mountain man who fastened down each night
with lists, proprieties, "what a woman does
or does not do," perpetual endings. Once,
a hawk snagged in his barbed wire fence.
It flailed like a fallen Icarus.
She cut it out.
Still over the pasture the mountains shone,
Sawtooth's white ladder, Audubon's,
above them the ever-moving stars
indifferent to all labels, maps.
            She left the bars up after her.

4.
Along the wave of a precipice
her thought ran like a ptarmigan,
mottled and still like the glacier scree.
Only the wing beat remembered,
hardly observed, invisible,
the sound of one hand, the thunder
of one breath.

These are the hills where woman has no name,
having communion with the trees
in their green study. Mountainous
the talking in the needles: Engelmann's,
jackpine, white bristlecone.

Avens and snow buttercup
profess immortal innocence.

The coney's house
(its bedding for its airing out)
might have been hers. Good housekeeping
is notice of fair weather.
High enough
the language of destruction fades. In mist,
in cloud, she walked in the original.

It was not to name the mountains she was there.
Even her cairns were secret: a hummingbird's
moss thimble, or
a white outcrop of lichen where her trail
turned by a star notch in the hill,
a windfall once a panther's cache, a broken rock,
broken, each winter, differently.
She knew the mountains as she knew
the compass of her kitchen, dark
(those cabin nights) but everything
in answer to the motion of her hands.
        to live in, the solution —
                nothing more.

5.
The swordsmen on her mantelpiece
have frosted a little in winter's light.
Their book-supporting scabbards fill with dust.
Over her pond the hungry deer
scatter their tiny hoofprints like grey hail.
The beaver's lodge
steams like a chimney in the dawn.
Someone is dreaming. The sky,
staining a little with ruddy snow

as if the sharp peaks cut it, glows
like a mirror. The sun ascends
corn maiden's ladder and the clouds
huddle like sheep for the shepherd's horn,
the wind that drives them from the peaks
to beat below the tree line, to subside
filling the unimportant trails,
blocking the skier's highway.

A vein bursts in the city's side,
sometimes: cloudburst. The prairie creek
stripes through the city, heaped with glass
and plastic rubbish, peters out
in vacant lots, in camping grounds,
in tales of desert drownings and flash floods.
Now, by the irrigation ditch,
brown waters draining from Cherry Creek,
her old car moves like a crippled toad.
Fumes from the city fog the peaks.
The sky is yellowed like stained, dead fur.
Car lights along the highways trim
the Front Range like a distant mall.
But she has slipped under the cottonwoods.

New Year's: all things must be unlocked,
left open a crack — front door,
back door, a window — so the stars
can coast in on their film of dust
and sail out with time's leavings. Shells
must break for hatching.
                    And his room
left roofless, wall-less, only frame

with one red, rusting bedsprings
is the room
where new constructions can begin —
building with sunlight,
starlight,
with spruce dust, sand, with lupine, and the pale
continual agitation of the green
and golden aspen, "shooting stars"
(the "twelve gods" of the swamp).

His ropes sat in the Mountain Club
for months. His boots
almost a year.
A use will be found for anything.

6.
We walk, sometimes, in the woodlot here
in this shabby eastern province where the bears
wander like ruined overcoats
in the city's unofficial dump.
There are old walls,
the last sites of lost farmlands, clay-filled holes,
pastures of alders and hackmatack
and roadbeds covered with bracken.
Every year
the place where the farm stood when we came
was and is now some rusted tin,
brambles, and something beneath the grass,
chassis perhaps, or a chimney stone — each year
this place is less a place.
We'll lose it soon,
tracking our way through the beggar's-ticks

and the drought-browned mosses on the stones.
"There's the wall," you may say. It's around here,
then.
      And so this night
I watched a sunset drain away
the colours from the city. Just at dusk
my pear and a maple after it
echoed in rose and scarlet shades
the sun's withdrawn circumference,
beating the gold leaves, shattering green —
and all that green and yellow have gone black.
Just here, where I hold the map
(light, candle, mind)
I see a rose shade glimmering —
pale rags strung on a ghost's twig arm —
to shake at the edge of my eyesight, almost there
and almost invisible —
so too what I think I remember fades:
it drains away.

Her cabin, this winter, all alone,
with the stuffed bear holding his valet tray,
the fireplace swordsmen cold as ice,
and the snow heaped over the window sills.
What sleeps in the cellar all this time
or stirs when stiff Orion stirs,
moving along the mauve spruce trunks
after the leaping, mad, white hares?

But here's the sun, rocketing over the aspen rods,
tipping the white cones of the firs
so each encrusted helmet slides

sinking the green ears further. Drip —
the moving needled waters prick the snow.
Plop — and the snow-plugged chimney top
releases its cap. Grey water runs
along the granite chimney stones
and pools below the andirons — wet coals
and soft, decaying ash
that like a compost of years past
hardens again, and night returns:
a whole world under glass.

The cabin is not empty. At the stove
her candle, ghostly, is a shaft
in moonbeams, or a spider web.
Her eyes are bright as an animal's,
the crystal eyes of the deer, the bear,
the wolf skin hanging on the wall.
The piercing rays from the third, wide room
open the snow, where her brother waits —
and the red springs of that empty bed
rusting past autumn.
          The chimney smokes with auroral fires,
blue as the tight buds of the firs,
sealed against wind, and the windows shake
reflecting the flat plane of the lake,
and the twins, congealed in the photograph —

but the imaginable warmth
of what is there,
                    is there . . . .

This Far

"A wild patience has taken me this far."
Adrienne Rich

The powerful
are sick with power, churn
like pebbles under water on a rock
and burrow their deep fathom.

The powerless
do not exist.
We all exist.
Our power is in time.

Even the dead are powerful.
The new-killed dog
raises its head from the grassy bank
where the young man lies,
where the neighbours talk above them,
looking away.
I heard the ambulance's whine
like summer night's mosquitoes.
On the road
the caterpillars hunched and died.
These grate my mind.

A wild
patience will take all of us,
each in the confines of our cell.
There is no single evil.
We endure,

and will be taken further
than this far.
Life's patience will outlast us,
even death's.

Ask

Why have you been calling an echo?
Only to hear what will not come? Beyond
your "wishing seat." the valley plunge
is streaked with browning grasses. A black bear
raises her head (your scent, perhaps?)
and, shucking your image from her, trots away.

And how your hands, chafed, and still awkward,
hold themselves, one to the other,
familiar as old friends
that do not need to speak!
Don't they still keep their distances?

The flat, bright stones
glisten with raucous lichens, orange and red.
The dried gauze of a flower head
drifts like a dust of spider at your feet.
Even the mica's busy. In the air
your thin voice hovers, fading.
Are you there?

In This Picture
(watercolour by Tanaka Bunsei, c. 1842)

A spider in its web: a scrap of sky
proves dangerous. Gold dusk
drenches the paper, and a bird
whose body is the air
sketches its hesitation.

The subject must be twilight.
That these things, or others, may occur
(bird flight, the spider's stasis)
are remarked. The ebbing light
is heavy, and the brush
that set the representation down
is set down too.
Sunset, an almost bird takes flight —
the mind, then, too.

Dormant

All roads are undiscovered now. The blaze,
privately hewed to the mountain top,
is bandaged with forgetfulness.
The present heals in winter and is past.
How could you burrow below the snow
finding a mouse path to her door
or glide above it like an owl,
your shadow knitting the twiggy trees
into a lace of winter time like a grey web
of losses, which are not, being the season's loss
and time's, but interstitial vapourings
closing, as the owl passes over them,
then opening out?

The Clouds

The clouds are the same on the hillside,
or almost the same.
We can not say nothing has changed,
and the clouds *have* changed on the hillside.

Hills vary, of course, and weather.
The ozone changes; earth's little ball,
this marble aggie for the thumb,
still takes its solar journey, but
something has changed.

A bell tings from the kitchen:
that's for time
    which we will not know change —

    nor solitude, however suns
    may twinge and glow;
    nor truth, which we will never own;
    nor beauty we can't measure,
    nor love
which in its showings changes like the flow
of story after story no One tells.

The clouds move over the distant hills
as they have done millennially;
their majesty
remains when we are sloughed away.

Nothing has changed; is changed,
is changing; loss
of what we know and love, the advents
of a newer loss, perverse
extensions of our hope.

An infinite, elastic space
expands between our solitudes.

It is almost the same.

The Red King Dreamed Me

The red king dreamed me.
I escaped
through a tiny crack in his red pate
like steam —
          No,
like the mouse
from under the throne in London
which that cat saw,
visiting the Queen,
who was the King
                    (as she sometimes is).
Did I dream him?

Did she, Elizabeth the King,
dream that confused, red dodderer?
Who was the cat?
Whose red eye glittered with desire?

I am the red king in my nap
among my antique battle plans
and she
who stood while dying that she die
standing.

I am what cowered beneath her skirts
and, too, that cool and classless
eye
that looked at her, as a cat may look,

and Alice, trudging towards the crown
across a grid of wargames.

The red crown looms above me.
My head swells,
grows feverish.
I have a splitting headache,
and I dream.

Coming Home

I found the traces where I'd been
like some discovered, alien land
in which my footsteps did not fit.
My bed
like an abandoned countryside
was winter white.
My shelves gleamed in the sunlight
like wet rocks.

As if I'd been a bird's nest which the snow
had filled and overweighted,
as if wind
had split the broken hollow to its hairs,
the thin grey grasses, spread them
so they swam
like motes in air —

I moved
in this clean

vacancy

which was my self.

No The About Him

The man is walking slowly in the rain.
The man requires
(from this particular window)
an umbrella, say, an epithet
to keep the generalizations off, at bay
     (to stab at swans?)

He's the man who was here the other day.
Half up the staircase, wasn't he?
He wasn't, but who wasn't there
is (from this window) only one
of any I might pick and choose

     (leaning over the window sill,
     stars in my bosom — the paper kind.
     Remember? The teacher glued them on
     to say "Good Girl," or, "Passable.")

The point (you thought I hadn't one)
is that the man is only from
this point of view the man.
He may be God-knows-Hoover from his own.
The "the" is only mackintosh,
a kind of wet apparel for wet days
you hang up in the restaurant
like the umbrella and forget.

Forget it right away. The the-man's dead.
The woman went before him with his lunch
(ants, sauerkraut, tofu, bread, wine)

making his way in the wilderness:
"Behold we are not Adam are not Eve!"

Drenched in our each particulars, no the,
no circumstance repeats.
What mama makes: unique each time —
new gents for her old genes.

Cliff Head

barren to all points of the eye
a flat field
barbered by bleaching space

a forty-foot drop
to the water

no jetty   no boat

and the sea floats by
without a hook to catch at it

and the grass

without a barn, no grazing stock, no long
red, rusting implement to hang
like a hand in the elements

Cliff Head:
an isolated house
as on a shelf

the paint's kept up —
someone lives there
but the doors are shut

and will not reach out

A Useful Leaf, This One
(a Japanese print)

A useful leaf, this one,
and I may as well use it,
being, for the moment,
a yellow bird.

I am no more
than a sensation in my feet,
an instinct to hold on —
one foot above the other —
to

a green stalk, hollow,
resonant —

through which the ticking of the soil
sings in the ticking of my veins
and in the clouds
that tick past over head.

Look:
the leaf is still quivering.

I am not there.

The Long Way Through the Chairs

The cat takes the long way through the chairs,
a shadowless embroidery of motion, past
the line between
two points, inobvious, subtle, intricate.

The purely sensual pleasure of the path
is a type of some rare poetry
which makes the way it got there more delight
than ever where it was or is.

It also is a type of life
whose virtue is not one still place
tucked in the warmth of your elbow, nights,
nor this which lies like ink upon the page,
which lies,

but truth
which endlessly dissolves,
inobvious, subtle, intricate, motion
its pure delight.

Not Quite There

A floater on the membrane of an eye,
a tear would almost drown him, but he stays —
never in focus, never in one place,
and never far.

At night, sleep swells him:
giant steps, the city streets
echo beneath his flapping arms,
a princely moth whose chrysalis
returns, rebinds. Day cribs,
crimps, cripples, with its truths
that will not wash.

This sad acquaintance correlates
no narratives.
Too close to be invisible, or clear,
a presence, an outlier, shade
on shadow, lost
in the uncentering of himself,
he floats upon the membrane of an eye.
A tear would almost drown him.

do not cry!

Old Sow

(a whirlpool off Deer Island)

Snow melts to sweat
  in this wide cat's cradle of water
    dawdling between these rocky shores
      with their sharp,
        steaming faces.

It's not two minds I have, but several.
  I am rooted in water, a swaying cup,
    anemone from black ice,
      white hair tentacled, my eyes
        blank as the Old Sow's, obstinate.

The Ear of the Bat

The bat's ear, so honed it hears
the changes ring among the leaves,
dew swelling, or the bones
that creak in a blue mouse wrist,
hears only sound.

                    But you
who hear by heart's analysis
creation chanting in one voice,
star-gnatted tentacles of dawn,
the cloudy seas, the spawning grounds,
the forms of summer shifting,
can hear time.

The turbulence of alphas without end
beats in your thumbs, defines
the losses and diminishments of love,
the deaths of each white, dazzling day,
returning, and still mourned.

Down

The owl's grove has been lumbered,
splintered apart, as if Goya's eye
had felled Olympus.

  Grey, striped wings
  cast their shadows like fishing lures
  across the surfaces of ferns,
  threading the dusk as if weaving it,
  conspirators,
  night spirits, answerers, whose notes
  encode the moon's crypt,
  predators —

Holding my heart in an owl's fist,
I saw my blood
dripping like jet beads on the moss:
a drawing in ink.
The shrivelled ferns
like ashes fluttered in that black wind.
Ignorance, madness, brutality:
a sketch. Some paper bones.
An owl's beak plunged
into the quick of middle night —

But the machines
like bomb blasts broke
those trees, those talons.
A drained cyst,
daytime, on the logger's road.

The gods are down.
Build over their palaces the church
of down, down, down,
and down.

The Speck

came over the long,
grey
wind-shorn hills
like a trinket loosed
from a long
dream,
like paper blown
or a white
toy.

Under the hovering
darknesses
of night,
of sleep,
of approaching storm,
came over the grey
crest:
dot,
a speck
whitening into
the dull ravines,
running like water:

a white horse,
its mane gone crazy.

The ocean
groaned,
rumbling beyond
the greynesses.

A petrel,
storm rider,
a white wing,
sailed on before us
and into the foam
its great legs
flailing.

Its white neck
flashed;
it was surf,
and the white foam
fell
and was scattered.
A crazy
speck

running across
the grey combers,
vanishing
into the distances
like a toy,
like a piece
of paper
blown
into a dream —
and out of it . . .

Grand Manan Ferry

At the mist edge of the farther isles
the sea was tawny as if light
crept underneath a curtain.

There were two or three ducks stage right,
eider, perhaps. They left.

We were cold as our styrofoam coffee,
almost asleep. The theatre
was empty.

      Then —
gull fanfare: a trawler!
birds littered its wake.

The ocean was fizzing with porpoises,
cartwheeling troupes
splashing, subsiding.

A steady whale
like a steam switcher in its yard
worked back and forth,
its geometric banners placed, dissolving.

Then the sun
wrinkled the silk edge of the set.
Applause was faint.
The audience had gone in.

We heard the harbour bleating. The first roofs
shone flatly, paper programmes. Stiff
as paint the lighthouse stood.
We disembarked.

Rose, 30" x 36"
   (a painting by Marjory Donaldson)

That white rose hard as Colville skin
   is love grown cold.

      Is rose made perfect,
         rose unrosed.

      — No smell, no sex —
   huge clock of faceless timelessness —

      Medusa head.

Mal de Cuisine

An office would be worse: the desuetudes
of desk and dust and carbon, idiocies
which must be done.

This is a private freedom, here —
the freedom of the sink,
abandoned island, no right way
to peel the carrots, the rich stink
of old necessities returned
three times a day.

Oh counters of conformed desire
and polyester holidays! Flights out
to quickfood, frenchfries, and motels!

The housewife labours for herself.
Who else? A cupboard clean, a spare
and solitary worship of the thing —

An egg, perfection — but the shell,
the dish, the burned toast crumbs —
A bird weeps out the window as it does
each spring.

To fly from here, to wallow in the wild
and find a clean world after me
to come back home to!
Everything

continues, more or less, the same.
It may be luck.
The day moves as you push it,
only just.

Local Suite

1. Riverside Drive

The wind's too rough for the sailboats.
A cormorant, starting to hang out its wings,
has had second thoughts. Pale mustard flowers
shake in the rocks and styrofoam
of the riverbank. A runner in red mittens
pounds on past.
                    At the armoury
boys play at soldiers. My small dog
noses the thawing ground. Her thick
coat flares like thistle seed.

2. Fredericton Junction

Last summer's cat-tails, shaggy in the rain,
and blackbirds; a shiny, plywood station —
a purring bus clogs the parking lot,
the driver's gone across the street
to the new café. In the waiting-room
a girl in a yellow slicker and a child,
too hot in a pink fur snowsuit.

The café sign says "Chili." "Well,
I've got beans," says the counter girl,
"What else does it take?" The bus driver tells her.
She's set for the day.

The rain lets up. My husband walks
beside the tracks like a signal man,
and the train looks round its corner, small,
yellow, perfectly genuine,
and right on time.

3. Roberta's Wood Path

Spruce seedlings, still too small for lights
at Christmas time, line the narrow path
the children take. (The grownups bow.)
Ground cedar overhangs
a doll's ravine.
(The patch of bluing scilla is a lake.)

The gardener marks her stations with tin tags:
bloodroot, trillium, shooting-star.
Above us squirrels in their choir stalls cry
and drop the stale, wild apples on our heads.

4. Picnic by the River Light

Near-sighted, the moose swam toward us.
Halfway across it saw us, blinked, and turned around.
We watched it wading the island. Later
we saw it stumbling in a patch
of carefully ranked young lettuces,
a kind of Peter, harder to evict.

5. *Officers Square*

With red salvia, purple petunias, orange
marigolds, a turquoise beaver pondering
its flat trough, and the plumbing-roofed
memorial like a bandstand.
The benches are red and yellow but the grass
has been left green.

The girls in their bare feet like it.
Stretched out flat, with their dress shoes
under their heads, they are getting
their lunch-break sunburns. Each
as pink as a rose.

6. Needham Street

Narrow, its dusk closed in with wires
as if to catch some late, hawk-watching pigeon.
A tiny, tidy house is dwarfed
by the massive, white datura bush.
The ancient, crippled apple-tree is
propped on crutches, a loyalist.
Hopvine, nightshade, half-wild cats,
the houses crowd the sidewalk, but
there is Boldon's light, a stained-glass window:
a beckoning cup, blue amber grail.
Against it the white budworm moths
flutter like cinders and beat the screen.

7. Loyalist Graveyard

Dust on the willows and raspberry briars,
and grey seed heads: angelica, milkweed,
virgin's bower — a sort of fog. The plot
might once have been bare meadow. Elms,
drawing their darkness like a hood,
have closed it in till it seems hardly large enough,
only by accident not forgot. The past
gets smaller the less we remember it.
This is almost *too* small.

8. Odell Park

The rags of this year's tartan come apart,
unroof the old farm's gravel road. The sun,
slanting between the tree trunks, looks
like the last of the tourists. It touches us,
lightly, its hands already cold.
There will be frost.

9. Burning the Greens

From the post-Christmas pyre of trees
speckled with tinsel, a steam of snow
dampens the smell of starter fuel.
A missed gold ball wags sadly. Flame
reddens the wet face of a child
slumped on his father's shoulders.
Soon the blaze
will send the old year toward the sun
we've not seen much of, lately. Dusk
happened at three. The bonfire's through
by bedtime. Like one small, red eye,
Mars dogs pathetic Jupiter.

10. *The Myth of a Small City*

The myth of a small city where,
on a snowy night,
it doesn't do to walk carelessly:

the walker behind you with lengthening tread
has raised his wooden hammer.

He is the clock of midnight, the bad turn
someone will do you, sometime.

By the wall, a shadow fidgets,
starts to run.

Rib

Do you divorce this tumour from your side?
this nagging clutter, this refrain
always to be come home to,
always the same?

So Adam had Eve outward, losing heart.

It is a strange courage you give me,
ancient scar.

Whale Watching

Kingfishers skymarked the jetty: the boat
lumbering in with its nursery blue
awning and chairs — and the sea pearl-grey
blending into a paler sky, the rocks
like charcoal glistening in the mist.

How slowly the islands drifted past!
How softly the water pebbled in our wake!
Fish, sometimes, a wheel of phalarope,
fog glistening on the railings — someone saw
a spout, a porpoise, a fish jump, wave break,
spot of white — a shadow, whether cloud or deep,
a silver shaft of evening wash the sea —
two crags hooked by their lighthouse and one pine,
one rope, one ladder, very neat —

    then we turned back river
and, close to land
with its toy Noah houses, minke lay
lolling in water like a dog
too lazy to bark, domesticate.
We all took pictures. We docked again.
And they were still there, still calling,
kingfishers, bright as rain.

On the Picture Sent to the Stars of a Man and a Woman

In the picture of the man and the woman sent to space,
she is not waving her hand.
Is she perhaps unsure
of what her greeting should be, what response?
She lets him take the risk
of his serene conviction
that what he thinks appropriate is true.

Is his hand raised to greet or strike?
That's not clear. Is she there
to receive whatever hand, making whatever gesture, points,
like God, creating Adam, points?
Or has she nothing to do with it?
    (Like Noah's wife
    carried on board against her will
    with all those mice and gerbils —
    needed, not
    yet listened to,
    supposing she thought of something she might say.)

She has the blank, retentive stare
of a cat surveying the neighbourhood.
She won't go out
until she's sure she knows what's there.
"Let dogs delight in bark and fight."
She'll speak
if there's something to say.

Or perhaps she is meant to say "Silence." That's
the message so far
from whoever we're sending our pictures to.
Perhaps she is only along for him:
"Men! Someone has to take care of them!"
Or perhaps she is only listening:

"Buddy up there (whatever you are,
whatever he says) you talk to me.
I'm listening."

Old House

> (for my friend who understands that I have
> remembered her story wrong)

There is still the great well
with the fig trees,
the pears, the apricots, the wild
sour cherries you loved so much —
in its solemn depths you sensed the sea
beating the avenues beyond.
                              The stairs
were outside, straight up to the roof
where you could lean against the stone
and gasp for stars
like fish looking up through water.

One Ramadan, the adults
shuttered below in their disciplines,
praying and wringing their hearts like cloths,
you, the bad child, innocent,
lay infidel in starlight on the roof

and saw
Mohammed — comet — shooting star —
crossing and entering heaven's door
that opens once —
                    a vision milled
from the stone wheel below you
grinding the pain of adult life
to its pure spasm —
                      that white splash
that bridged the sky's dome was their cry.

The garden is there, in the city, still,
with its great, stone well
green with the trickles of old wars.
It is you who cry now, in the shuttered house,
while the children go up, midnights, for the stars . . . .

Somewhere I Have This Headache

Blasting,
or armies practising,
some small dull thunder punctuates,

disrupts the easy swelling
of the light
like a weak throbbing in a vein.

Somewhere I have this headache.

The rock ledge pulses on my house.
The full
gelatinous spring weather roils

the filthy streets,
the gritty air, my
sinuses.

Is this artillery, or
just some common blasting?
But so long
they keep it up!

No roads are going through
just now.
Some building I don't know about?

Or just some practice bombing?

Underneath
the lenten stupor of the day
reverberates some stupid speech:

"defence"
by killing all the earth,
that sort of thing.

The trees, too cold to put out buds,
are shivering, a little.

So am I.

Grey Mare

"the Anglo-Saxon resistance to theory"
B. Godard

Grey printed words
last longer than a horse's heart,
longer than yours, grey mare,
whatever they know of earth or plough,
or the soft warmth of the little cat
that sleeps along your spine cold nights,
or the voice of the farmer's wife at noon
as she strokes your nose.

Machines
do beautifully whatever they do; and you,
too, suffer, rust, and die. Theory
is neither plough, machine, or horse,
nor guarantee of spare parts should
some unforeseeable small thing
break down. There will be
other theories, new, every spring,
with the Easter births.

Who fusses over theory
who has one silky, nuzzling colt?
There is no news
in what continues to be true.
We use what we find we can,
grey mare.

Prospero on Setebos

Largely alone on this dry beach
where only my shadow waves at the sea —
(for the trees are shaking mindlessly,
an echo to the thunder of the air —
they do not, like green pennants, flap
assertive meanings as I would, if only
in the closing of my eyes) —
I am much plagued by demons:

mine, my own, my little spawn
that scuttle — roaches under leaves,
petty luxuries of angst,
or self-indulgent wastings of old spleen —
The air paints on its surfaces
my shadow waggling like a leaf,
transports me into exile: here
and nowhere, which this is.

I want to rise, to shake the sand
off from my knees, hold out my hands
to the whistling torrents, bless
the whelm-resounding universe
as if I had created it.
But all my spirits, prisoned
like lamed flies, I tamed,
I lamed; they cripple me.

What should I do? Oh yes,
should write. Something,

What was the message, sir?
Who should I ask? I am bemused,
bermudaed — all this calm
beats on the shore a fishy sea.
All that comes up will go down again.
The spirits whittle at my ears.
Time makes all musics plain.

Is What We Have

These metaphors are an injury.
I am not white sand
poured through a Cretan hourglass.
These images, these moons, hetairas, geishas,
these crippled folktale animas —

are like oil stains in water,
thick, stinking, and undrinkable — in light
a rainbow answering the sky's,
but false —
it makes no promises.

As at the bottom of the well,
where the green sides
put out a waving feather of dark brown
dissolving into the water's root,
nothing is pure. We drink
the water the past passed.
A certain wetness stains our teeth.

I could drink fire
and join the burning of the stars
beyond all sexes sexual, as god is,
or the fiery mind.

We hold, in our stale, plastic jugs,
water from a shadowed well. Sip
carefully! The water, like the wetness

of our words, is what we have.
It will not be
unchanged by us.

The Bone Arch

There is no home, no hearth,
no central place
the mind can slip to, settle in,
as if it were a bed, a nest.
It's all pretend.

The bindweed in the path,
the burst vein in the widow's eye,
your friend who yesterday was glad
of your unfeigned attention — each
has spirals and complexities, a different map
and compass, each a trip
that journeys out away from you.

The stars move, fidget, and the skin
turns colour, and the bones
shift and arrange themselves towards age.
All that is known fans out from us
like a slow yacht's expanding wake
that crosses grey horizons and is gone.
The museums of our memories, the springs
that were forever fertile, perfect dawns
too well remembered, have passed on.
Though we stand still the minutes move.

In Joseph's chapel by the ruins
where they found Arthur, Guinevere,
or some gold-hilted Saxon and some hair,
a whale's jaw holds the tussocked earth
as if it were appointed for that task.

What did the dumb cetacean know? Was it not more
to God's and Nature's glory that it leaped?

My flesh is cast
upon the waters of my days,
and my words rot.

The Rookeries

The rookeries gabble and grieve at the sea,
rainbow-backed, treacherous, innocent.

Out of such chick squeal distinguish a voice
both tragic and comic the water makes
thundering over them: no two alike.

An infinite grain fingers over them, eyes
on the wounded, forgives them:

the goney impaled on the trap rock, ants
and the fruit flies of summertime suck him.

Along the white edge of any strand
a tepid feather, a dropped soul,
the grey epistles of the crowd . . .

early around to the outer shove,
backing, backing, almost the edge —

Where are the feathers of this long thing,
this infinite, grieving, and fluttering thing?
No two alike.

Adrenalin

Good Doctor R.,
high as a child, unable to come down —
adrenalin emergency keeps him alert beyond
all need.
   Your kindly man
runs violent in place, fuelled fool,
his tongue
    pulse mad.

So nature churns.

As a young dog guarding an empty house
crashes against a window pane,
or a humming bird's red, burning coal
traverses continents twice yearly, so
You burn, dear God, some mortals at full blast.

You ravish him.

On some such run,
driving against Your deathly hand,
ducking along the mountain tops,
all of his little plane on fire,
You send him blazing like a star
and humming like a bobbin in Your mill
to piece Your wounded chaos, knit him in,
married to air.

Your evening then
grows smooth,
            effacing,
bland.

Mortuary Figure at the Fogg Art Museum

There you are in stone
with your puppy dog,
a dead bird dangling from your hand.
I'm sorry. Only a little girl
and all of your life ahead of you.

Noisy, oh I am sure you were.
This disappointment was the first
of many that never came to you.

In the lobby the potted lilies bloom,
austere designs. On the white tiled floor
muddy footprints. The fretful whine
of a bored child wriggling from a hand.
Too cross to kiss. Too cold.

In the Garden of Mildewed Roses

In the garden of mildewed roses
the roses' blowsy heads
bobbed in the currents of the fog
like wood buoys in the harbour.

There were seals
or kelp heads in the bay.
I could not see,
but sat down by the roses in the wet.

They smelled good, greyed
and rotting as they were.
Self-pity — like rain,
I was drenched in it.

The usual, petty vanities:
to speak, and not be listened to;
to stand, and not be spoken to;
to walk home in the darkness by myself
while in among the hedges groups of friends
or new acquaintances vivacious
with their inquiries
rattled like migratory birds!

Yet what I wept for was not true.
I had been heard. And spoken to.
I had a friend to go home to.
I went. A real friend doesn't have
to be right there. And even out of reach

she can be found.
At the end of a letter. A long thought.

I publish to the world and make my points
small as a cat's marks on the rug.
A long trudge, maybe.
A lifetime's work.
Such a little scrawl!

A whole life spent on poetry!
I feel like a bird in an aviary
with a small voice —

or like these roses with their scent,
this huge hillside of roses where just one
sad lover of all flowers sits
so wet with personal concern
she scarcely lifts their petals to inhale.

These fogs will lift,

the seawinds show
beyond the bay the mountains of the heart!
Let me bloom, razzle, go to seed,
as time permits, ungrudgingly!
The garden of all flowers is hereabouts.

Watercolour
　　　by Aunt Margaret

Aunt Margaret's road
is not one she ever went out on,
you'd judge,
though there are those deep ruts in it.
Her dawn
might be the sunset,
red, white, blue,
striped like a banner.

At the back
her bushes draw themselves up close,
a wilderness
that might be just the neighbour's farm.
You could walk there;
you wouldn't much.

But Margaret
didn't stay at home. She taught.
She sent her sibs to school
with money she earned teaching.

Her claustral, rural road
that seems to stop up short in bush
below an emblematic sky
seems like a duty to stay put.
No option, not, at any rate,
one that you'd take.

Mottos

1. The tallest tree is the first one felled,
    but the pulp mills will keep grinding.

2. If you want an answer you must accept delivery.

3. God has no pride.

The Poem Insists

I'm almost invisible, almost
inaudible, running below your feet like mud.
(And you have such thick boots on!)

I'm all over the place,
pulling the streets down, ripping the marsh.
I drip down your walls.
I ooze in place.

You veil me out with rubber sheets.
You insulate.
You wrap your air in plastic bags.

I am
the cinders on your fixtures, the grey stuff
that clings to your attic vents. I am
a message someone is sending you.

Slip. Slop.
The wet dog brings me in.
You throw her out.
I go out clinging to her fur,
but I'll be back.

You grab your mop.

It Moves

The light on a crow's wing briefly
slides as light on water slides.

A sea beast gathers to a knot
and inks an instant on the sky,
high leaping, falling —

or a feather,
dropped from a crow's wing, strokes the air.

Motion is half the message.

If the sea,
bundling and swaying beneath these words,
has anything to say, it's that.

si muove

Fog

The fog coming up the cliff onto the dry grasses
hangs on the rose heads. Fir cones and red leaves
in the grass, sorrel, I think, or strawberry, and twigs,
red also, the light in them shifting about. The water drags
the petals down. So it drags me. It drags
the seeping hours of the day.

Why should the heart lie dormant, stunned,
as if swallowed up by the icy fog?
The cliff tops nod and turn away — seals, they are seals —
or the ragged foot
of an osprey or —
nothing at all.
The water swirls, lapping against the muddy cliffs,
reiterates. Always the same old water. Fog.

Nothing's Insured

A white weed, skinny in a darkened thatch
of woodlot roadside, reaches for the light
(the thrust that "drives the cherry")
and the wind
keeps talking, but this drought,
however temporary, temporal,
or local, will insist.

The weed sinks into gravel, and the wind,
still babbling, grazes it
(the wind
that strokes the gravel of the moon) —

The flower we never saw (I mean
the one we did not name, the one
we did not pick, press, dry, and glue
to a botanic label) like
that gnat nooked in its labellum
will die.

Meanwhile,
we savour albums of the auk, make soup
from yellow photographs
of trees more old than nations, cut
for things we can't find when we look.

But then,
what did we think would last?
Nothing's insured.

Pelagic

The last frond of the gulf stream uncurls here,
touching with temporary green
the lichened, battered island.
A reindeer's breath
clings to the cliffs.
A people might survive
here, so a cairn suggests.
Nothing is easy. Don't look behind.
Something is always coming — ghosts,
or a great swelling in the sea,
or famine, in the pale form of a beast.

Just over the ridge is winter hall,
snowy forever. The pack ice
jostles and squeaks like lumpish birds
while the sea keeps beating
its white rocks.
The coast line fractures at a touch.
Nothing is sure — except the sea:
slick surfaces monstrous with patternings
changing, unsafe, and restless —
on which indifferent bosom
a bird sleeps.

Dear Tiger

*"The happiest women, like the happiest nations,
have no history."*

George Eliot

1.

I was a perfect picture then. I breathed
the summer of perfection. I was five.
The painter was my papa's friend.
We walked in the public gardens every day.
The fountains made a gentle noise
like mama's skirts.
You can see in the picture: my blue dress,
the curls they cut off later — she would wind
them round her finger with the comb.

There were lilacs and poppies like soft balloons,
and I, as tender silky as the rose
that, faded from the opera bouquet,
lay in its gilt posy rim
limp as the fish that papa caught
which leaped a little in the grass
like rainbows, then grew dim —
they wilted, bent their rosy heads
into the basket's lettuces —
I shone.

The fever came.
The heat came in from the dusty trees
and soured the white-washed nursery.
The white sheets prickled me like briars.
They cut my papa's favourite curls and dried
white towels upon my head. I dreamed,
and saw the fountains leaping in the park,
making no noise, and I went to them.
And in this silent picture I awoke.

2.

At sixteen I made my classmates each
a valentine — a poem, a drawing —
whimsical, romantic, as
each one might like, so everyone,
even the ones who had no friends,
would get one, unsigned valentine.
A secret. No one guessed.
(A quiet girl like me!)

I didn't mean them all to guess,
though Mother thought they ought to have.
I think it made her angry.
How she would feel, now,
that you do not even know my name,
holding my album in your hand!
But after all, how could you know?
You are not kin.

I took my album south with me
when I married.
I didn't write my friends' names in,
though I wrote
"Dr. Williamson" on Father's, since it looked
so stern (he was never stern!)
and on the little drawing of
"The beautiful Miss Helen Jones"
who was my best friend ever —

It was after the War. Dr. Falligant
studied homeopathic medicine
under Father, and he asked for me.

So handsome, so truly considerate!
Father said I was too young;
they could not bear
to part with me.

Three months —
but Father never could say no
too long, to me. I was
your great-great-grandfather's
first wife. I died
in giving birth to a dead child.
He will never have mentioned me.
I left my album for you, dear.

(unsigned)

3.
I stood straight as a soldier
when Daddy was
the Brigadier.
I sent the Royal War College
his papers in a shoebox.
Do you know,
they never even acknowledged it?
I think the silly fellows have
mislaid it.
But they sent
me an invitation to their mess.
The Prince was there.
He does not hold himself as well
as Daddy did, but better than
these men you see upon the streets
these days, slip-slop.

When Blackie died
Daddy would never have another dog.
We never had cats.
But if they want to visit me —
like Tiger. I knew who owned him.
He'd come in for his tea
and go out again. When his family
were all away they'd leave him out
and he'd come right in
and sleep all night at the foot of my bed.

He was a soldier, Tiger.
He grew old.
One day a new tom on the block
came in our yard and fought with him.
By the time I got a bucket of water out
to throw over them
it was too late.
There were bits of Tiger everywhere.

I went out this morning for raspberries
(Daddy loved them so)
and slipped
on the porch steps and fell.
I lay with my face on the gravel path
and I thought of Tiger,
dear Tiger.
It must have been almost a year
after that terrible, terrible fight.
I lay with my face on the gravel path,
and I thought of dear Tiger.

Protext

Imagine a text that does not cling to any of those capitalized nouns that zoo about in the pages of tidy-minded professors. A text that does not interpret, describe, express. A text for which reality is only the texts among which it takes its existence, striking off small flashes of delight at every touch — much like a firefly leaf to leaf. A text of partial similes, allusions, puns, and anagrams — fluid rather than rigid, a crossword of cloud-shapes, inventive, casual. A text of texts.

Of old texts which, half-forgotten, floating in the skies, have figures we no longer see. Of fairy stories, of ballet, of opera, and of cinema. Above all of the theatre, its artificialities so matter-of-factly impermanent, all paper, tinsel, masquerade —

and yet demanding an assent (our fingers crossed). The cardboard ship can float if we believe it floats.

If we concede we don't know where we are going, why do we insist upon having a map? a plot? some prehistoric form? Is there an author for our play? Is someone piloting our ship? Is the river itself, that milky way, flowing up as well as down? Or is it never the same river, and only flowing out?

Who's being conned? How much of any disbelief can we believe? There is nothing under the masks, we are told, not even ourselves. We are all dissolved. Scene after scene each life becomes a Trivial Pursuit.

But poetry can not tell us that. Sails set, the poem carries us. We're here. We are not lost.

You Go On

I would like to sit on the bridge and watch
the pelican, for a while, as he sits there
with his beak tucked in.

The river slides under my feet and out to the rim
of the grass-ridged bay.

Look down the piles
at the oysters, clinging like brown rags.
Yet the water's clear.

And the pelican
will shake himself loose from his statue's pose
and fly across the marshes, still
with his shoulders hunched.

I've seen him land
on water with his toes spread wide.

The fish
will come up river soon.

The sky's gone grey beyond White Bluff.

The pelican
has a simple notion of his own
business he will be working on. I'm here,
third post from the bank, on the down-stream side.

If I come back empty-handed, never mind.